Contents

THE ANGEL GABRIEL

The angel Gabriel was sent by God to the town of Nazareth, in Galilee, to visit a girl called Mary. Mary was promised in marriage to a man named Joseph, of the family of King David.

'Greetings, Mary! God has blessed you,' said the angel Gabriel. 'God has chosen you to do something very special.'

Mary was surprised and a little afraid of the angel, and she was anxious about what his message could mean.

'There is nothing to be afraid of, Mary. This is good news. You are to have a baby, a son whom you will name Jesus. There will be no one else like him. He will be great, the Son of God, and he will rule over a kingdom that will never end.'

'But I have no husband yet,' said Mary. 'How can I have a baby?'

'The Holy Spirit will make this happen,' the angel answered. 'Even your cousin Elizabeth is expecting a baby and everyone thought she would never have children. Nothing is impossible for God.'

'I am here to serve God,' Mary answered. 'I am ready for whatever he wants me to do.'

Then the angel Gabriel left her.

Mary visits Elizabeth

Mary was so excited by the news the angel had given her that she prepared to visit Elizabeth in the hill country of Judea.

As soon as Mary greeted her, Elizabeth's baby moved inside her and the Holy Spirit told her the news that Mary had brought to her.

'Bless you, Mary! And bless the baby you are carrying inside you,' said Elizabeth, hugging her. 'I can't believe how lucky I am to have you visit me, you who are to be the mother of my Saviour. You have believed what God has told you and you have been willing to serve him. People will remember this for ever!'

Then Mary answered her.

'I will praise God with all my heart! I am so happy because of what God has done for me — a girl, no more special than any other. For ever after people will say how blessed I am because God has chosen me to serve him by giving birth to his Son. God is great and kind and merciful! He cares about the poor and needy and gives them all they need.'

Mary stayed in Elizabeth's home for three months before returning to her home.

THE JOURNEY TO BETHLEHEM

Around this time, Caesar Augustus, the Roman emperor who ruled the land, decided that a census should be taken of the whole of the Roman world. It meant that everyone had to return to the land of his ancestors to be counted.

Mary and Joseph had to travel from Nazareth to Bethlehem, because Joseph belonged to the family of King David.

By now, Mary was expecting her baby. It was a long journey on foot for a pregnant woman, but they joined the crowds of other people who were all travelling to Bethlehem to register as they were.

No room at the inn

Bethlehem was larger than the hill town of Nazareth, where Mary and Joseph were living, but it was not a very large town. The streets were crowded with all the people who were visiting for the census, as well as those who lived there. Roman soldiers marched among the visitors, who moved quickly out of their way.

Mary was tired. She knew that soon her baby would be born. Joseph was anxious for her, wanting to find somewhere safe and warm for the birth, but there were too many people. There was no room at the inn.

THE BIRTH OF JESUS

The pains began that told Mary that it was time for her baby to be born.

That night, Mary gave birth to her first-born son. As Joseph could find no other place for them to rest, she made a bed for him in a manger, among the hay put there for the animals. She wrapped him in the strips of cloth she had brought with her, and placed him in the manger to sleep.

A HOST OF ANGELS

Shepherds were out in the fields that night, watching over their sheep. Suddenly, an angel appeared in the darkness and light shone all around them, so that they were terrified.

'Do not be afraid,' said the angel. 'I bring you good news, a cause for great celebration for everyone! A baby has been born today in Bethlehem who is Christ, the anointed one, come to save his people. You will know when you find him because he is wrapped in strips of cloth and lying in a manger.'

Then a great number of angels appeared, praising God. 'Glory to God in the highest heaven, 'and peace to men on earth.'

SHEPHERDS
FIND THE BABY

Gradually, the sound of the angels disappeared and the sky was dark and silent once more.

'Let's go to Bethlehem,' the shepherds said to one another. 'Let's go to see this amazing thing for ourselves.'

They left their sheep on the hillside and went in search of the new-born baby. Soon they found Mary and Joseph, and the baby, who was lying in the manger, just as the angels had told them.

When they had seen him for themselves, they went away, telling everyone who would listen that the special baby, Jesus, the anointed one, had been born and was there in Bethlehem.

Mary said nothing. But as she watched her baby son sleeping, her heart was heavy with the amazing things she had seen and heard that night.

A visit to
King Herod

When Jesus was born in Bethlehem, Magi from the East saw a new star in the night sky. They followed the star till they came to Jerusalem. They found their way to the palace where King Herod lived.

'Where is the child who has been born king of the Jews?' they asked. 'We saw the star announcing his birth in the East. Now we have come with gifts to worship him.'

King Herod was not happy to hear their news. There could be no other king while he was alive! He called together the chief priests and teachers of the law, and asked them where the prophets had said Christ was to be born.

WISE MEN WORSHIP

When the Magi left the palace, they made their way to Bethlehem, following the star they had seen in the East. When it seemed to stop over a house in Bethlehem, they were overjoyed.

They left their camels and went into the house, where they found a young child with his mother Mary.

They knew at once that they had come to the right place, and knelt and worshipped him. They brought him the gifts they had carried from their homelands, treasures of gold, incense and myrrh.

The Magi did not return to Jerusalem, but went back to their own country another way, having been warned in a dream not to go back to King Herod.

THE FLIGHT INTO EGYPT

After the visitors had left them, an angel appeared to Joseph in a dream.

'You must get up,' he said, 'and go with the child and his mother to Egypt where you will be safe. King Herod will know that he has been tricked and he will search for the child. He will not rest until he has killed him. Stay in Egypt till I tell you to return.'

So Joseph got up straight away and left before morning, taking with him Mary and the little boy, Jesus, to safety.

The rage of King Herod

King Herod waited day after day for the return of the Magi from the East.

When he realised that they were not going to return, he was furious. He calculated the age that the child would be from the times given to him by the Magi, then he gave orders for all the little boys in Bethlehem under two years old to be killed.

There was great weeping and mourning among the families in Bethlehem, but Jesus remained safe in Egypt.

A home in Nazareth

Some years later, King Herod died. An angel appeared once more in a dream to Joseph.

'Get up,' said the angel. 'Take the child and his mother and return to your home. The people who wanted to take his life are dead. It is safe to go back again to the land of Israel.'

Joseph knew it was time to go home. He took Mary and the child back to Israel and they made their home in Nazareth in Galilee.

Jesus grew up strong and healthy and learned the carpenter's trade from Joseph, until the time came for him to do the work that God had given him to do.

Bible stories can be found as follows:

The angel Gabriel, Luke 1:26-38

Mary visits Elizabeth, Luke 1:39-56

The journey to Bethlehem, Luke 2:1-5

No room at the inn, Luke 2:3-4, 7

The birth of Jesus, Luke 2:6-7

A host of angels, Luke 2:8-14

Shepherds find the baby, Luke 2:15-20

A visit to King Herod, Matthew 2:1-4

Wise men worship, Matthew 2:9-12

The flight into Egypt, Matthew 2:13-14

The rage of King Herod, Matthew 2:16-18

A home in Nazareth, Matthew 2:19-23

This is a 3C Publishing book
First published 2010
This edition 2010
3C Publishing, Sky House, Raans Road, Amersham, Bucks,
HP6 6JQ, UK

ISBN 978 1 906842 20 8

Copyright © 2008 Anno Domini Publishing
www.ad-publishing.com
Text copyright © 2008 Rhona Davies
Illustrations copyright © 2008 Tommaso d'Incalci

Publishing Director Annette Reynolds
Editor Nicola Bull
Art Director Gerald Rogers
Pre-production Krystyna Kowalska Hewitt
Production John Laister

Bristish Library Cataloguing in Publication Data
A record of this book is available from the British Library
All rights reserved

Printed and bound in Singapore